# WOODY GUTHRIE

## ROLL ON, COLUMBIA ◆ The Columbia River Songs

ISBN 978-1-4950-6313-8

TRO ESSEX
MUSIC GROUP

EXCLUSIVELY DISTRIBUTED BY

HAL•LEONARD®
CORPORATION
7777 W. BLUEMOUND RD. P.O. BOX 13819 MILWAUKEE, WI 53213

Visit Hal Leonard Online at
**www.halleonard.com**

# Introduction by Bill Murlin

I t was an odd professional combination by today's standards: a Dust Bowl-born radical songwriter and a North west-bred federal power agency. But when Woody Guthrie joined up with the Bonneville Power Administration in 1941, creative sparks flew. Call it luck or genius. It was probably both.

Woody Guthrie was hired when the BPA asked Alan Lomax, then head of the Folk Archive at the Library of Congress, to recommend a folk singer who could write songs for a proposed film documentary that would appeal to the people and promote development of the Columbia River and hydro-power. The songs could also help sell bonds for creating public utility districts. Lomax suggested Guthrie could write all the songs needed. Having just returned to the west coast with his wife and three children, following a year-long, unhappy flirtation with financial success on New York City radio programs, Guthrie was now broke, out of work, and available. Luck and genius rolled together.

Though the job was supposed to have lasted a year and include on-camera appearances, by the time Guthrie got to Portland the BPA folks realized there was too much red tape involved and cut the job to a month. For those 30 days, Woody toured, wrote, typed and sang. His creative turbines spun at full capacity as he witnessed first-hand the ways irrigation and hydro-electricity could elevate a hardscrabble life for so many, particularly the farmers living in the Northwest. "He drives out to the construction sites. He sits on the banks watching the skilled workers with the bulldozers and jackhammers. Talking with the men in the bars after work or at lunch hours, trying to get their lingo down right. And with all that rattle and roar around him, he's writing down one verse after another." (Pete Seeger) Woody himself wrote, the pictures and words from those trips were "faster to come and dance in my ears than I could ever get them wrote down." Genius.

Woody stated repeatedly that he wrote 26 songs while in Oregon. The sound track in the 1949 documentary The Columbia included only three of them. In succeeding years, about a dozen Columbia River songs were published in albums or songbooks and some became famous. The rest disappeared.

Nearly four decades later, I came to work at the BPA, with a long back-ground of folk music involvement and a news reporter's curiosity. Woody's name and voice in the documentary movie told me there was more to the story. The remnants of his personnel papers left in Portland were teasers.

Historians and I rummaged through old papers and federal archives seeking Woody's lyrics. Appeals to former employees and an avalanche of news media coverage produced long-forgotten acetate disk recordings. Chalk up many of these discoveries to luck – the right people in the right place at the right time. And saving Woody's federal personnel file from the shredder was pure fortune.

We discovered there were, indeed, 26 songs, some of which had never been seen nor heard until all the recovered lyrics and transcribed recordings were published in 1988. Identifying melodies for some of the lyrics got a big boost from Pete Seeger. Genius.

Woody Guthrie, Roll On, Columbia, The Columbia River Songs contains the original versions of all the songs Guthrie submitted to the BPA in 1941. He did change some of the lyrics when selected songs were first published in his own songbooks and albums. Additionally, Woody's actual recordings of the songs, as they appear on the Rounder Records recording, do not always follow either the original version nor the published version as Woody was famous for never singing a song the same way twice! That's the 'folk process' and Woody was one of its masters.

The BPA honored Guthrie by naming a substation for him, which remained for 45 years. Now, thanks to my former BPA teammates, Woody's contributions are forever secured, as a few of his Columbia River lyrics and writings are now carved in stone within the dedicated Guthrie Circle at the entrance to the BPA Portland headquarters. I'm proud to have been a part of reviving this unique collection and preserving a special slice of Northwest history. And while the movie The Columbia has been relegated to relative obscurity, Woody's Columbia River songs are part of the Pacific Northwest heritage. Their musical electricity is still heard, and people who've never seen the Columbia River sing about it. That's Woody's genius – writing poetry that endures and songs that stick to the tongue.

*My kudos to folklorist Hobe Kytr and Sarah Smith of BPA for their creative writing, from which many of these thoughts were edited. Kytr introduced the 1988 publication of this songbook. Smith's essay appears in the BPA book, "Power of the River." "Woody Guthrie, Columbia River Collection" (1987) CD is available on Rounder Records. The 2000 documentary film "Roll On, Columbia" is now available on DVD. Both are available at the Woody Guthrie Store, WoodyGuthrie.org*

# TABLE OF CONTENTS

# ROLL ON COLUMBIA, ROLL ON

"Roll On, Columbia"
Words by Woody Guthrie
Music based on "Goodnight Irene"
by Huddie Ledbetter and John A. Lomax

**VERSE:**

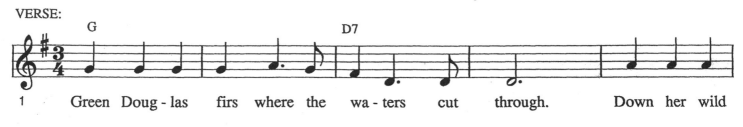

1 Green Doug - las firs where the wa - ters cut through. Down her wild

6 moun - tains and can - yons she flew. Can - a - di - an North - west to the

11 o - cean so blue, Roll on, Co - lum - bia, roll on!_____

**CHORUS:**

17 Roll on,____ Co - lum - bia, roll on. Roll

22 on,____ Co - lum - bia, roll on. Your pow - er is turn - ing our

27 dark - ness to dawn, So, Roll on, Co - lum - bia, roll on!_____

Other great rivers add power to you,
Yakima, Snake, and the Klickitat, too,
Sandy, Willamette, and Hood River, too;
Roll on Columbia, roll on!

Year after year we had tedious trials,
Fighting the rapids at Cascades and Dalles.
The Injuns rest peaceful on Memaloose Isle;
Roll on, Columbia, Roll On!

Editor's Note:

This verse was added later by Michael Loring, BPA, 1947.

Tom Jefferson's vision would not let him rest,
An empire he saw in the Pacific Northwest.
Sent Lewis and Clark and they did the rest;
Roll on, Columbia, Roll On!

At Bonneville now there are ships in the locks,
The waters have risen and cleared all the rocks,
Ship loads of plenty will steam past the docks,
So, Roll on, Columbia, Roll On!

And on up the river at Grand Coulee dam,
The mightiest thing ever built by a man,
To run the great factories for old Uncle Sam;
It's roll on, Columbia, roll on!

It's there on your banks that we fought many
  a fight,
Sheridan's boys in the block house that night,
They saw us in death, but never in flight;
Roll on, Columbia, Roll On!

Our loved ones we lost there at Coe's little store,
By fireball and rifle, a dozen or more,
We won by the Mary and soldiers she bore;
Roll on, Columbia, Roll On!

Remember the trial when the battle was won,
The wild Indian warriors to the tall timber run,
We hung every Indian with smoke in his gun;
Roll on, Columbia, Roll On!

*Note: The chorus of this song can be sung after every verse, or after every two or three verses, as you like. This song was wrote up by an Oakie passing through your country, and I'm pretty certain that everybody just first a coming into this country has got some such similar song in his or her head, but times is such that they just can't sing it out loud so you might not hear it.*

*Woody Guthrie, outskirts of Portland, Oregon, 5-12-1941.*

# ROLL, COLUMBIA, ROLL

Words and Music by Woody Guthrie

C capoed to 5th fret

1. There's a great and peac-ful ri-ver in a land that's fair to

see, where the Doug-las fir tree whis-pers to the snow-capped moun-tain

breeze. The cliffs are so-lid gran-ite and the val-ley's al-ways

green, this is just as close to hea-ven as my trav'-lin feet have

CHORUS:

been. Roll Co-lum-bia won't you roll......, roll......,

roll......, Roll Co-lum-bia won't you roll......, roll......, roll........

Stand upon her timbered mountain, look across her silver strand,
See the crops and orchards springing to the touch of nature's hand.
And it's further up the river where your eye will meet the skies
Where you'll see the steel and concrete of the big Grand Coulee rise.

Chorus

There at Priest and Cascade rapids men have labored day and night,
matched their strength against the river in its wild and reckless flight.
Boats and rafts were beat to splinters but it left men dreams to dream
Of that day when they would conquer the wild and wasted stream.

Chorus

Uncle Sam took up the challenge in the year of '33
For the farmers and the workers and for all humanity.
Now river you can ramble where the sun sets in the sea,
But while you're rambling river you can do some work for me.

Chorus

Now there's full a million horses charged with Coulee's 'lectric power
Day and night they'll run the factory and they never will get tired.
Well a coal mine gets dug out and an oil well it runs dry,
But Uncle Sam will find his power where the river meets the sky.

Chorus

# RAMBLIN' BLUES
## (Portland Town)

"Ramblin' Blues (New York Town)"
Words and Music by Woody Guthrie

I come from Louisiana where the Red Fish in the bay;
I come from Louisiana where the Red fish in the bay;
Lord, I come from Louisiana where the Red Fish in the bay;
And it's hey, hey, hey, hey!

I said, which a way does Columbia River run?
I said, which a way does Columbia River run?
I says, a which a way does Columbia River run?
From the Canadian Rockies to the ocean of the Settin' Sun.


I walk down th' road and I see your Bonneville Dam;
I walk down th' road and I see your Bonneville Dam;
Walk th' rocky road and I see your Bonneville Dam;
'lectricity run th' fact'ry makin' planes for Uncle Sam.


Well how many rivers have you got in Portland town?
I said, How many rivers have you got in Portland town?
I said, How many rivers have you got in Portland town?
They said, The Columbia River is the river that they all run down.


Oh, Columbia River, takes 'em all to the ocean blue;
That Columbia River, takes 'em all to the ocean blue;
That Columbia River, takes 'em all to the ocean blue;
Snake, Hood, Willamette, Yakima, and th' Klickitat, too.


I'm a ramblin' man; and I ramble all the time;
I'm a ramblin' man; and I ramble all the time;
I'm a ramblin' man; and I ramble all the time;
But every good man has got to ramble when it comes his time.


I'm out of work, ain't a working, ain't got a dime;
I said, I'm out of work, ain't a working, ain't got a dime;
Yes, I'm out of work, ain't a workin', ain't got a dime;
But a hard workin' man gets it down and out some time.


Well, when I seen that great big Bonneville Dam;
It was when I seen that great big Bonneville Dam;
Yes, when I seen that great big Bonneville Dam;
Well I wish't I'd a been workin' makin' somethin' for Uncle Sam.


I had a job last year, but I ain't had a good job since,
I had a job last year, but I ain't had a good job since,
I had a job last year, but I ain't had a good job since,
I'll get a job along the River just for Uncle Sam's defense.


I never took relief, but I need relief right now;
I never took relief, but I need relief right now;
I never took relief, but I need relief right now;
But me an' th' River's gonna roll roll along somehow.

# PASTURES OF PLENTY

Words and Music by Woody Guthrie

1. It's a might-y hard row that my poor hands have hoed,

My poor feet have trav-elled a hot dust-y road,......

Out of the dust bowl and west-ward we rolled,...... And your

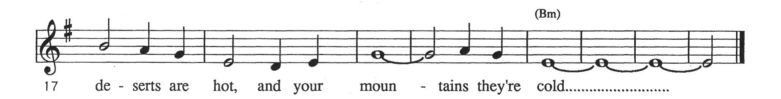

de-serts are hot, and your moun-tains they're cold.........................

I worked in your orchards of peaches and prunes,
And I slept on the ground 'neath the light of the moon;
I picked in your cotton, cut grapes from your vine,
And I set on your table your light sparkling wine.

We travel with the wind and the rain in our face,
Our families migrating from place unto place;
We'll work in your beet fields' till sundown tonight,
Travel 300 miles 'fore the mornin' gets light.

Arizona, California, we'll make all your crops,
It's northward to Oregon to gather your hops;
Strawberries, cherries, and apples the best,
In that sunshiny land call'd the Pacific Northwest.
It takes home loving mothers and strong hearted men;
Every state in this Union us migrants has been;
'Long the edge of your cities you'll see us, and then,
We've come with the dust and we're gone in the wind.


I picked up a rich clod of dirt in my hand,
I crumble it back into strong fertile land;
The greatest desire in this world that I know
Is to work on my land where there's green things to grow.


I think of the dust and the days that are gone,
And the day that's to come on a farm of our own;
One turn of the wheel and the waters will flow
'Cross the green growing field, down the hot thirsty row.


Look down in the canyon and there you will see
The Grand Coulee showers her blessings on me;
The lights for the city for factory, and mill,
Green Pastures of Plenty from dry barren hills.


It's always we've rambled, that River and I,
It's here on her banks and I'll work till I die,
My land I'll defend with my life if needs be;
'Cause my Pastures of Plenty must always be Free!

Editor's Note: The verses above are as they appear in the
original BPA manuscript. The following verses were added in the
commercially recorded or printed versions of the song.

I've wandered all over your green growing land,
Where ever your crops are I've lent you my hand,
On the edge of your cities you'll see me and then,
I come with the dust and I'm gone with the wind.


Green pastures of plenty from desert ground,
From the Grand Coulee dam where the waters runs down,
Ev'ry state of this Union us migrants have been,
We come with the dust and we're gone with the wind.


*From the collection of Woody Guthrie, Professional Oakie, just a passin' through*

# ELECKATRICITY AND ALL

Words and New Music Adaptation
by Woody Guthrie

I love a long - shore - man, I do, ma - ma; I

love a long - shore - man, I do, ha - ha!.... We're

gon - na get mar - ried,... we are, ma - ma, And we'll

have e - leck - a - tri - ci - ty and all,....... We'll

have e - leck - a - tri - ci - ty and all........

He held my hand, he did, mama,
He held my hand, he did, ha ha,
We're gonna have children around our door,
And have eleckatricity and all.


We walked on the seashore, we did, mama,
We walked on the seashore, we did, ha ha,
He whispered and told me the way it would be
To have eleckatricity and all.


He combed my hair, he did, mama,
He combed my hair, he did, ha ha,
He said it would wave when we get settled down
And have eleckatricity and all.


He hugged me tight, he did, mama,
He hugged me tight, he did, ha ha,
He said he would hug me morning and night
When we have eleckatricity and all.


He kissed my lips, he did, mama,
He kissed my lips, he did, ha ha,
He said that he'd kiss me a million times
When we get eleckatricity and all.


I'm going to tell papa, I am, mama,
I'm going to tell papa, I am, ha ha,
He might not like it but I don't care

'Cause we'll have eleckatricity and all.

# MILE AN' A HALF FROM
# TH' END OF TH' LINE

## (End of My Line)

Words and New Music Adaptation
by Woody Guthrie

Verse

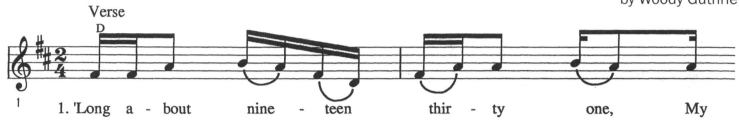

1. 'Long a - bout nine - teen thir - ty one, My

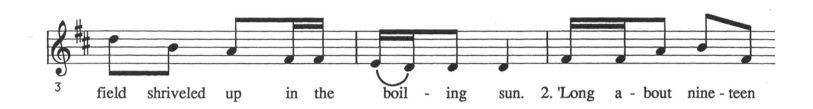

field shriveled up in the boil - ing sun. 2. 'Long a - bout nine - teen

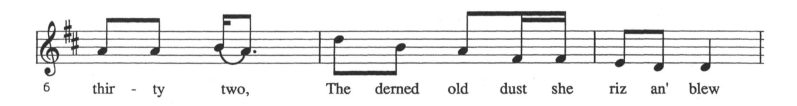

thir - ty two, The derned old dust she riz an' blew

Chorus

End o' my line, end o' my line, I

reck - on I come to the end o' my line. End o' my line,

end o' my line, I reck - on I come to the end o' my line.

Editor's Note: The BPA version starts with these two verses

It was a curious an' terrible pain
Tryin' to make a livin' on th' Northern Plains;

Settled them plains in '89,
Twenty-five years we done just fine.

'Long about nineteen thirty one,
Field shriveled up in the boiling sun.

'Long about nineteen thirty two,
The derned old dust she riz an' blew.

'Long about nineteen thirty-three
A workin in the dust was a-killin' me.

Long about nineteen thirty-four
The dust it riz and blowed some more.

Figgered I'd leave 'bout every day,
But the wife she'd pray and beg me to stay.

In the fall of 1935,
It blowed my crop about nine miles high.

Early nineteen thirty-six,
Me an' my wife in a devil of a fix.

Chorus: Me an' my wife in a devil of a fix.
        Me an' my wife in a devil of a fix.

'37 the dust it stopped,
But the god dam hoppers got my crop.

'38 was a dusty year
An' I says, woman, I'm a leavin' here.

19 hundred and thirty-nine,
We fanned our tails for the Oregon line.

Chorus: Fanned our tails for the Oregon line.
        Fanned our tails for the Oregon line.

We got a-hold of a piece of land,
Fifteen miles from the Bonneville dam.

Bonneville dam's a sight to see,
Makes this e-lec-a-tric-i-tee.

'Lectric lights is mighty fine,
But I'm just a mile from the end of the line.

Milk my cows and turn my stone,
Till the Bonneville folks they come along.

My eyes are crossed, my back's in a cramp,
Tryin' to read my bible by my coal-oil lamp.

Oregon state is mighty fine,
If you're hooked on to the power line.

But there ain't no country extry fine,
If you're just a mile from the end of the line.

End o' my line, end o' my line,
I reckon I come to the end o' my line.
End o' my line, end o' my line,
I reckon I come to the end o' my line.

# HARD TRAVELIN'

Words and Music by Woody Guthrie

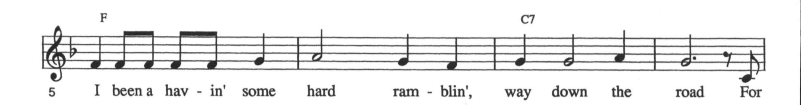

Yes, I been a havin' some hard travelin'
    Way down the line
O well, it looks like a job of work
    Is sho' hard to find.
I been down the highway gadin'
Job a huntin' and a boom a chasin'
    I been havin' some hard travelin' Lord.

Well, I been a hittin' them big orchards
    Back down the way
Yes, I been a missin' a might good job
    Most ever' day;
I been a livin' on jungle stew
It's now boys, I'm a' tellin' you
    I been a havin some hard travelin' Lord.

I been a grubbin' that truck gardenin'
    Not far from here
I been a grabbin' at spud 'taters
    Fourteen long years;
I been a pickin' yo' beans and peas
Way down upon my knees,
    I been a havin, some hard travelin' Lord.

# A RAMBLIN' ROUND

Words by Woody Guthrie
Music based on "Goodnight Irene"
by Huddie Ledbetter and John A. Lomax

1. Ram - bling a - round your ci - ty, ram - bling a - round your

town; I ne - ver see a friend I know as I go ram - bling a -

round, boys, as I go ram - bling a - round.

My sweetheart and my parents
I left in the old home town,
I'm out to do the best I can
As I go ramblin 'round boys,
As I go ramblin 'round.

I make the fruit and harvest
And follow them up and down,
But I caint save a nickel,
As I go ramblin 'round boys,
As I go ramblin 'round.

The peach trees they are loaded,
The limbs are bending down—
I pick 'em all day for a dollar,
As I go ramblin 'round boys,
As I go ramblin 'round.

Sometimes the fruit gets rotten
And falls upon the ground,
There's a hungry mouth for every peach
As I go ramblin 'round boys,
As I go ramblin 'round.

I wish that I could marry,
So I could settle down—
But I caint save a penny
As I go ramblin 'round boys,
As I go ramblin 'round.

My mother prayed that I would be
A man of some renown.
But I am just a railroad bum
As I go ramblin 'round boys,
As I go ramblin 'round.

My sister and my brother
Would both be mighty proud
If I could get a job of work
And quit this ramblin 'round boys.
And quit this ramblin 'round.

# NEW FOUND LAND

Words and Music by Woody Guthrie

17    liv - in' in the light of the    morn - ing,    Liv - in' in the light of the    morn - ing.

I built me a house of a new-cut tree,
A new-cut tree, a new-cut tree.
I built me a house of a new-cut tree,
I'm a livin' in the light of the morning.

I lit my lamp with a new-found light,
A new-found light, a new-found light,
I lit my lamp with a new-found light
And I'm a-livin' in the light of the morning.

I'm plantin' my feet in the new-dug ground,
The new-dug ground, the new-dug ground.
I'm plantin' my feet in the new-dug ground.
I'm livin' in the light of the morning,
Livin' in the light of the morning.

I brought my child from my new-found wife,
My new-found wife, my new-found wife,
I brought my child from my new-found wife,
Livin' in the light of the morning,
Livin' in the light of the morning.

Well I just got up to my new-found land,
My new-found land, my new-found land.
I just got up to my new-found land,
I'm livin' in the light of the morning,
Livin' in the light of the morning.

# OREGON LINE
## (That Oregon Trail)

Words and Music by Woody Guthrie

Chorus:
I'm gonna hit that Oregon trail this comin' fall
I'm gonna hit that Oregon trail this comin' fall
Where that good rain falls a plenty
Where the crops and orchards grow
I'm gonna hit that Oregon trail this comin' fall.

Well, my land is dry and cracklin'
And my chickens they're a cacklin'
'Cause this dirt and dust is gettin' in their craw
They been layin' flint rock eggs
I got to bust 'em with a sledge
I got to hit that Oregon trail this comin' fall.

Chorus

Yes, my hogs and pigs are squealin'
They're a rockin' and a reelin'
'Cause there ain't no mud to waller in the draw
I'm gonna grab them by their tails
Take them down that western trail
I'm gonna hit that Oregon trail this comin' fall.

Chorus

Well, my good old horse is bony
And he's tired and lonesome too
You can count his ribs three quarters of a mile
Throw my bedrool on his back
Both the bay horse and the black
I'm gonna hit that Oregon trail this comin' fall.

Chorus

Now, my true love she gets ailin'
When this dry old dust gets sailin'
And she wishes for the days beyond recall
If we work hard there's a future
In that north Pacific land
I'm gonna hit that Oregon trail this comin' fall.

Chorus

*This song, the words and music, were composed by W.W. (Woody) Guthrie, not at my home but on the high banks of the Columbia River, for the Department of Interior, Bonneville Power Administration, 811 Northeast Oregon Street, Portland, Oregon, on the fourteenth day of May, in the year of Nineteen hundred and Forty One.*

# OUT PAST THE END OF THE LINE

Words and Music by Woody Guthrie

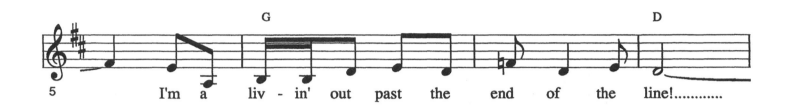

I can hear that Columbia River Roll,
    I can hear that Columbia River roll,
    I can hear that Columbia River roll, Lord, Lord,
But it don't bring no power to my door.

I'm a farmin' man, I work hard all the time,
    I'm a farmin' man, I work hard all the time,
    I'm a farmin' man, I work hard all the time, Lord, Lord
And I shore need a little power from your line.

Well, I milk my cows and chickens, too,
    Yes, I milk my cows and chickens, too,
    O yes, well, I milk my cows and chickens, too, Lord, Lord,
and I shore need a kilowatt or two.

My land's a crackin', Lord, my field is dry,
    My land's a crackin', Lord, my field is dry,
    My land's a crackin', Lord, my field is dry, dry, dry,
But I cain't get no water up so high.

I use an old smokin' lantern all the time,
    I use an old smokin' lantern all the time,
    I use an old smokin' lantern all the time, time, time,
'Cause I'm a livin' out past the end of the line.

They tell me Bonneville is a'comin' down th' line
They tell me Bonneville is a'comin' down th' line
They tell me Bonneville is a'comin' down th' line, line
And it's a good thing they got here just in time.

I reckon hard luck brings good luck sometime, time, time,
    I reckon hard luck brings good luck some time,
    I reckon hard luck brings good luck some time, time, time,
So you can shoot your power down my line.

Now my children won't run away to town,
    My children won't run away to town,
    My children won't run away to town, town, town,
Since Bonneville brung the 'lectric lights around.

Well, my whole family'll quit this a-runnin' around,
Yes, my whole family'll quit this a-runnin' around,
Yes, my whole family'll quit this a-runnin' around, 'round, 'round,
Since Bonneville brung that 'lectric power 'round.

# IT TAKES A MARRIED MAN TO SING A WORRIED SONG

Words by Woody Guthrie
Music traditional ("Cannonball Blues")

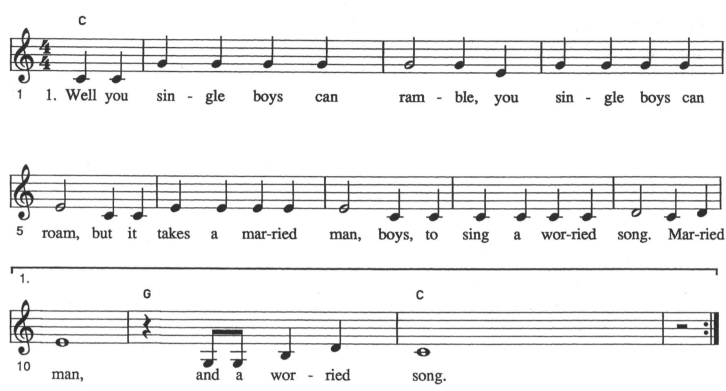

Chorus:
I'm a married man, I sing a worried song.

It was once I used to ramble, and I sung a single song,
But it's now that I am married, boys, I had to change my tune.

Chorus:

I was rough and I was rowdy when I led a single life
But I got to take it easy since I got myself a wife

Chorus:

I have got six little children to feed and educate
And it's really got me thinking, not a nickle on the place,

Chorus:
I'm a married man, I sing a worried song.

I am very happy married and I got to save my dough
We have got six little children and expecting several more,

Chorus:

Yes we got six little children, and expecting several more
Kids run out like cattle when you open up the door.

Chorus:

Yes you single boys can ramble and can lead a rowdy life
But you'll have to take it easy when you get yourself a wife

Chorus:

You will have a flock of children and have others coming on
It takes a married man, boys, to sing a worried song.

Chorus:

*Woody Guthrie*
*12-20-40*
*New York City*

# THE BIGGEST THING THAT MAN HAS EVER DONE

## (The Great Historical Bum)

Words and Music by Woody Guthrie

I worked in the Garden of Eden, 'twas in the year of two,
Join'd the apple pickers union, I always paid my due;
I'm the man that signed the contract to raise the rising sun,
And that was about the biggest thing that man had ever done.

I was straw boss on the pyramids, the Tower of Babel, too,
I opened up the ocean, let the migrant children through;
I fought a million battles and I never lost a one,
Well, that was about the biggest thing that man had ever done.

I beat the daring Roman, I beat the daring Turk,
I defeated Nero's army with thirty minutes work;
I stopped the mighty Kaiser, and stopped the mighty Hun,
And that was about the biggest thing that man had ever done.

I was in the revolution when we set the country free,
Me and a couple of Indians that dumped the Boston tea;
We won the battle at Valley Forge, and battle of Bull Run,
And that was about the biggest thing that man had ever done.'

Next we won the slavery war, some other fella and me,
And every slave in Dixie was freed by Robert Lee;
The slavery men had lost the war, the freedom men had won,
And that was about the biggest thing that man had ever done.

And then I took to farming on the great midwestern plain,
The dust it blowed a hundred years, but never come a rain'
Well, me and a million other fellas left there on the run,
And that was about the biggest thing that man had ever done.

I clumb the rocky canyon where the Columbia River rolls,
Seen the salmon leaping the rapids and the falls;
The big Grand Coulee Dam in the state of Washington
Is just about the biggest thing that man has ever done.

There's a building in New York that you call the Empire State,
I rode the rods to 'Frisco to walk the Golden Gate;
I've seen every foot of film that Hollywood has run,
But Coulee is the biggest thing that man has ever done.

Three times the size of Boulder or the highest pyramid,
Makes the Tower of Babel a plaything for a kid;
From the rising of the river to the setting of the sun,
The Coulee is the biggest thing that man has ever done.

I better quit my talking 'cause I told you all I know,
But please remember, pardner, wherever you may go,
I been from here to yonder, I been from sun to sun,
But Coulee Dam's the biggest thing that man has ever done.

There's a man across the ocean, boys, I guess you know him well,
His name is Adolf Hitler, We'll blow his soul to hell;
We'll kick him in the panzers and put him on the run,
And that'll be the biggest thing that man has ever done.

# BALLAD OF THE GREAT GRAND COULEE
## (The Grand Coulee Dam)

Words and Music by Woody Guthrie

1. Now the World has sev - en won - ders that the

trav - 'llers al - ways tell, Some gar - dens and some

tow - ers, I guess you know them well. But

now the great - est won - der is in Un - cle Sam's fair

land. It's the King Co - lum - bia Riv - er and the

1-7

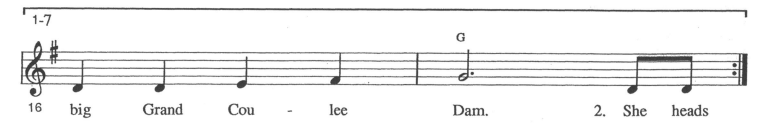

big Grand Cou - lee Dam. 2. She heads

18   big   **GRAND**   **COU - LEE**   **DAM**..........................

She heads up the Canadian mountains where the rippling waters glide,
Comes a rumbling down the canyon, to meet the salty tide,
Of the wide Pacific Ocean where the sun sets in the west,
And the big Grand Coulee country in the land I love the best.

At the Umatilla Rapids, at The Dalles, and at Cascades,
Mighty men have carved a history of the sacrifices made,
In the thundering foaming waters of the big Celilo Falls,
In the big Grand Coulee country that I love the best of all.

She winds down the granite canyon, and she bends across the lea,
Like a prancing dancing stallion down her seaway to the sea;
Cast your eyes upon the biggest thing yet built by human hands,
On the King Columbia River, it's the big Grand Coulee Dam.

In the misty crystal glitter of the wild and windward spray,
Men have fought the pounding waters, and met a watr'y grave,
Well she tore their boats to splinters and she gave men dreams to dream,
Of the day the Coulee Dam would cross that wild and wasted stream.

There at Bonneville on the river is a green and beautiful sight,
See the Bonneville Dam a rising in the sun so clear and white;
While the leaping salmon play along the ladder and the rocks,
There's a steamboat load of gasoline a-whistling in the locks.

Uncle Sam took up the challenge in the year of thirty-three,
For the farmer and the worker, and all of you and me,
He said roll along Columbia, you can ramble to the sea,
But river while you're rambling, you can do some work for me.

Now in Washington and Oregon you hear the fact'ries hum,
Making chrome and making manganese and light aluminum,
And the roaring flying fortress wings her way for Uncle Sam,
Spawned upon the King Columbia by the Big Grand Coulee Dam.

*From the collection of Woody Guthrie, Just Migratin' Through.*

# GRAND COULEE POWDER MONKEY

Words and New Music Adaptation by Woody Guthrie

Just tell me, little feller, what might be your trade?
Just tell me, little feller, what might be your trade?
I'm a feather man and a chinker, and a powderman from A to Z.

I could use a good mucker, I could use a good climber, too;
I could use a good mucker, I might put on a climber, too;
So, if you could climb and muck, I guess maybe I could use you.

No, Captain, I'm not a climber, I'm not a mucker, neither one'
Captain, I'm not a climber, not a mucker, neither one;
I was holdin' a stick of dynamite in my hand the day-day I was born.

I heard yer lowboss tell the flunky, you need a powderman bad;
I heard yer lowboss tell the flunky, you need a powderman bad;
I wanta show that Spokane girl just how ta lay this mountain down.

I snatched bolls way back thru Georgia, dipped sheep in big Montan;
Snatched a boll back in Georia, dipped sheep in big Montan;
Tryin' ta beat my way with a case of TNT to yer Grand Coulee dam.

Bossman, bossman, bossman, if ever the champion powderman you see;
Bossman, bossman, bossman, if ever the champion powderman you see;
Yer lookin' at him right this minute, 'cause that champion powderman is me.

Come here, Mister powder, lemme see how straight ye drill a drill;
Tell that Powderman come over here, lemme see him drill a drill;
Lemme watch him drop off a cliff or two, to help me fill my fill.

I drilled a million holes and I drilled my holes all night;
I drilled a million holes and I drilled my holes all night;
I filled my fills and I tamped all my fuses down tight.

I waited a minute for that sun to light up my sky;
I waited a minute for that sun to light up my sky;
I pushed down on my handle and I raised thr country ten miles high

Ten miles high, and when she settled back down still;
Ten long miles high, and when she settled back down still;
The marble was finished and loaded and the loose dirt filled in the fill.

Loose dirt fell down and made a whole new rivers bed;
Loose dirt fell down and made a whole new rivers bed;
Cap'n yelled: "I'll give ye the job." But I was buried way down dead.

# JACKHAMMER BLUES

## (Jackhammer John)

Words and New Music Adaptation by Woody Guthrie

I was borned in Portland Town,
Built ever port from Alasky down;
    Lord, Lord, well I got them Jackhammer Blues.
Built your bridges, dug your mines,
Been in jail a thousand times,
    Lord, Lord, well I got them Jackhammer Blues.


Jackhammer, Jackhammer, where you been?
Been out a chasin' them gals again;
    Lord, Lord, Well, I got them Jackhammer Blues.
Jackhammer man from a Jackhammer town,
I can hammer on a hammer till th' sun goes down,
    Lord, Lord, well, I got them Jackhammer Blues.

I hammered on th' Boulder, hammered on th' Butte,
Columbia River on a Five Mile Schute;
    Lord, Lord, well, I got them Jackhammer Blues;
Workin' on the Bonneville, hammered all night,
A tryin' to bring th' people some electric light,
    Lord, Lord, well, I got them Jackhammer Blues.


I hammered on Bonneville, Coulee, too,
Always broke when my job was through;
    Lord, Lord, well, I got them Jackhammer Blues.
I hammered on th' river from a sun to sun,
Fifteen million salmons run;
    Lord, Lord, well, I got them Jackhammer Blues.


I hammered in th' rain, I hammered in th' dust,
I hammered in th' best, and I hammered in th' worst;
    Lord, Lord, well, I got them Jackhammer Blues;
I got a Jackhammer gal just sweet as pie,
And I'm gonna hammer till th' day I die,
    Lord, Lord, well, I got them jackhammer blues!

*I wrote my first Jackhammer Blues when I was a livin' in a little old hotel up in New York Town, and the boys was a takin' up the pavement just below my window; but here it is set to a little faster time, and cut in one of the farthest, youngest, hardest working countries you ever seen, in the rough and tumble valley of the big Columbia River, out here in the good old Pacific Northwest, Oregon.*

*Woody Guthrie*
*This song written May 12, 1941*

# THE SONG OF THE GRAND COULEE DAM

## (Way Up in That Northwest)

Words and Music by Woody Guthrie

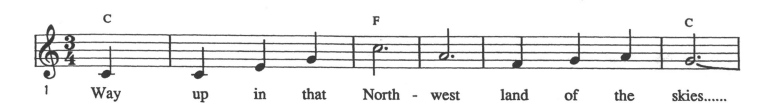

Mountain to Mountain all covered with snows,
I'll follow that River wherever she goes.

Winter and summer, springtime and fall,
She makes her way down her high canyon wall;

Bright rippling waters, sparkling so bright,
Seldom you see such a beautiful sight.

It's ninety-two miles northwest of Spokane,
There you will see her Grand Coulee Dam;

Woodwork and steel, and cement and sand,
Biggest thing built by the hand of a Man.

Power that sings, boys, turbines that whine,
Waters back up the Canadian Line:

400 miles of waters will stand
Rich farms will come from hot desert sand.

Flood waters lift up canyons so steep,
Making a lake eight hundred feet deep;

Waters will roll to the north and the south,
Never again be 'fraid of the drought.

Waters will flow with the greatest of ease
A hundred miles west, boys, and hundred miles east;

Factories that work for Old Uncle Sam
Run on the power from Grand Coulee Dam.

Ships on the ocean, ships in the skies,
Inch after inch her waters will rise,

High line will top your mountains and hills,
Driving your shop, and factories, and mills.

Niagara Falls send mist to the sky,
But Grand Coulee Dam is just twice as high,

She's forty-three hundred feet crost her top,
Five hundred and 50 down her rock.

I'll settle this land, boys, and work like a man,
I'll water my crops from Grand Coulee Dam,

Grand Coulee Dam, Boys, Grand Coulee Dam,
I wish we had a lot more Grand Coulee Dams

# COLUMBIA'S WATERS

"Columbia's Waters"
Words and Music by Woody Guthrie

1 "Good morn - ing,......... Mis - ter Cap - tain!".........

4 ....... "Good morn - ing, Man!" I'm just a strang - er,

7 trav - el - in' through your land;................ Do y' need a right good worker

11 ........ On your big Grand Coul - lee........ dam?

I'd like to settle down, but I ramble all the time,
I'd like to settle down with this woman and kids of mine,
But a place to settle down, Cap, is a pretty hard place to find.

I like to work and I work every time I can,
And I got a callous in the palm of both of my hands,
Ramblin' around from place to place is hard on a family man.

I like to work, 'cause I aint a gonna beg and steal,
Th' more I'm, a workin', boys, the better it makes me feel;
But my wife an' kids gets jubious ever time they miss a meal.

I'm a hard rock man, and I come from a hard rock town,
Back in my home town I was a man of some renown;
When I take a jackhammer down in a hole, gonna be some rock come down.


That Columbia River rolls right on down the line,
And the Columbia Waters taste like sparklin' wine;
But the waters in the dust bowl tastes like piclin' brine.


The money that I draw from a workin' on the Coulee Dam,
My wife will meet me at the kitchen door a stretchin' out her hand;
She'll make a little down payment on a forty acre tract of land.


We'll farm along the River and work from sun to sun,
I'll walk along the River and listen to the factories run,
I'll think to myself, Great Goodness, look what Uncle Sam has done.


Take some snow from off the mountain, mix it with some rain,
Take some metal from the mountain and melt it up again,
Stir it up with Power from Coulee Dam, and you got a big bombin' plane.


Take some waters from the valley, mix it up with snow,
Take a ramblin' family, just a travelin' down this road,
Mix it up with sunshine, and you ought to see the green things grow.


Standin' on a mountain lookin' out across the sea,
Columbia River is a mighty pretty sight to see;
Gonna settle down and live my life by the C-O-U-L-double E!

# COLUMBIA TALKIN' BLUES

## (Talking Columbia)

Words and Music by Woody Guthrie

Down a-long the ri- ver just set- tin' on a rock,

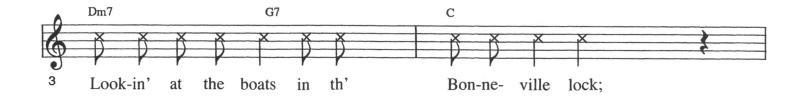

Look-in' at the boats in th' Bon-ne- ville lock;

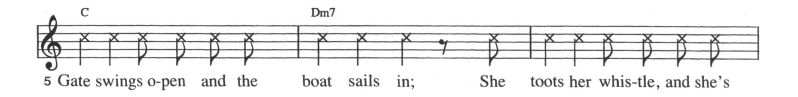

Gate swings o-pen and the boat sails in; She toots her whis-tle, and she's

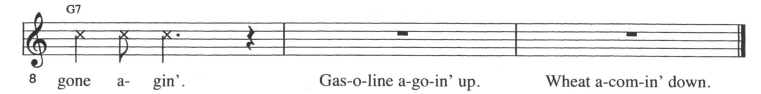

gone a- gin'. Gas-o-line a-go-in' up. Wheat a-com-in' down.

Down along the river just a settin' on a rock,
Lookin' at the boards in the Bonneville lock;
Gate swings open, and the boat sails in;
She toots her whistle, and she's gone again.
　　Gasoline is going up. Wheat a coming down.

Lots of folks around the country, politicians and such,
Said the old Columbia wouldn't never 'mount to much;
Times a coming, and it won't be long,
Till you're a gonna see that there's somebody wrong.
　　Thousand years. All this here water just a going to waste.

Filled up my hat brim, drunk a little taste,
Thought about a river just a going to waste,
Thought about the dust, thought about the sand,
Thought about the people, thought about the land.
Folks a running around (over creation).
　　Looking for a little place ... (something to do.)

Editor's Note: The following verse was added to the recorded version of the song. It was not written into the manuscript.)

Water come a splashing through the dam,
Trickling out across the land;
Power house sings and th' generator whines,
And down the hill comes a big power line.
       'lectricity runnin' all around ... Cheaper than rainwater.


Fellers back east they done a lot of talking,
Some of them a-balking, some of them a-squawking,
But with all of their figures and all their books,
Them boys didn't know their Royal Chinooks.
       (Salmons ... that's a) Good river. Needs some more (a couple more dozen)
big (power) dams on (scattered up and down) it. (Keepin; folks busy.)


Well, I pulled out my pencil and I scribbled this song,
Figgered all of them salmon just couldn't be wrong,
Them salmon fish, is pretty shrewd,
They got senators and politicians, too.
       Just like a president. Run every four years.


You just watch this river, and pretty soon,
Ever'body's a-gonna be changin' their tune.
The big Grand Coulee and the Bonneville Dam,
Run a thousand factories for Uncle Sam.
       Everything from fertilizer to bombing planes. (And ever'body else
       in the world ... makin' ever'thing from sewing machines to fertilizer ...
       atomic bedrooms ... plastic! Ever'things gonna be plastic.)


Uncle Sam needs houses and stuff to eat.
Uncle Sam needs wool (metal), Uncle Sam needs wheat,
Uncle Sam needs water and power dams,
Uncle Sam needs people and people needs land.
       Don't like dictators ... but the whole country'd ought to be run by electricity.

Editor's Note: In the BPA recording of this song, this last line was greatly modified:


I don't like dictators much myself, but this whole Pacific Northwest
Country up in here ought to be run, the way I see it, by E-Leka-Tris-I-Tee!
This same 'lectricity oughta jump, 'n sparkle, 'n jump, I think,
'round the whole world.

Editor's Note: At the end of the sixth verse, Woody probably never recorded the words "Everything from fertilizer to bombing planes." The words in parentheses are as-performed in the BPA recording of the song; there are other variations. In the talkin' blues style more than any other, Woody seemed to adhere to his dictate, "A folk singer never sings a song the same way twice."

# WASHINGTON TALKIN' BLUES

(Talking Dust Bowl)

Words and Music by Woody Guthrie

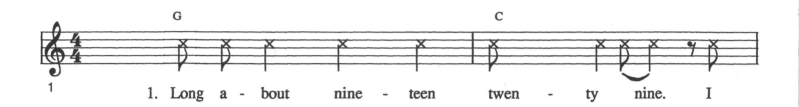

1. Long a - bout nine - teen twen - ty nine. I

owned a lit - tle farm, was a do - in' just fine. Raised a lit - tle row crop raised some wheat

Sold it ov - er at the coun - ty seat, Drawed the mon - ey. Raised a fam - ily.

But the dust came along, and the price went down,
Didn't have the money when the bank come around;
Tumble weeds and the black dust blowed,
So we hit the trail to the land where the waters flowed,
    Way out across yonder somewheres.

Well, the hot old rocks and the desert sand
Made my mind run back to the dust bowl land,
But my hopes was high and we rolled along
To the Columbia River up in Washington.
    Lots of good rain, Little piece of land. Feller might grow something.

We settled down on some cut over land
Pulled up brush and the stumps by hand.
Hot sun burnt up my first crop of wheat
And the river down the canyon just 500 feet.
        Might as well of been 50 miles. Couldn't get no water.

We loaded our belongings and we lit out for town
Seen the old vacant houses and farms all around,
And folks a leaving out, if you're asking me
That's as lonesome a sight as a feller can see.
        Good land. Grow anything you plant, long as you can get the moisture.

I struck a lumber town and heard the big saw sing,
And when business is good, why lumber's king;
I went to lookin for a job but the man said no,
So we hit the skids on the old skid row.
        Traipsing up and down. Chasing a bite to eat. Kids hungry.

Heard about a job, so we hit the wheat
Made about enough for the kids to eat,
Picked in the berries, gathered in the fruit,
Hops, peaches, and the apples, too.
        Slept in just about everything except a good warm bed.

Been to Arizona, been to California, too,
Found the people was plenty but the jobs was few;
Well maybe it's like the feller said,
When they ain't enough work, well, business is dead,
        Sorta ailin'. Ain't no money a changin' hands, just people
        changing places. Folks wastin gasoline a'chasin' around.

Now what we need is a great big dam
To throw a lot of water out acrost that land,
People could work and the stuff would grow
And you could wave goodby to the old Skid Row
        Work hard, raise all kinds of stuff, kids, too. Take it easy.

# THE TALKIN' BLUES

Words and Music by Woody Guthrie

Now if you want to get to heaven let me
tell you what to do
Just grease your feet with a little mutton stew,
And slide out of the devil's hand,
Just OOze over into the promised land.
    But take it easy — go greasy.

Standing in the corner by the mantle piece
Up in the corner by a bucket of grease —
I stuck my foot in that bucket of grease
And went a slippin' up and down
th' mantle piece —
    A huntin' matches, cigarette stubs,
    chewin' tobacco.

I was down in the hen house the other day
To hear the hens a singing, and the rooster pray,
The old hens clucked and the pullets called,
And the Shanghai Rooster baptized 'em all —
    Down in the horse trough. Dollar a head.

I went out a hunting and I took my dog
He treed a 'possum in a holler log —
'Possum growled and the dog he run —
I went back home without either one.
    Still hungery. Nothin' to eat in th' house.

I got a wife and a bunch of kids,
Always thought I'd count 'em, but I never did,
Some of 'em's eight, some of 'em's nine,
Some of 'em is hers, and some of 'em is mine.
    Mighty good workers when you get 'em
    woke up.
Corn huskers. Cotton choppers. Fruit jar masons.

The land around here's mighty poor,
We don't own the place no more —
You work all year on a place like this,
And you ain't got change for fifteen cents.
    This land is so poor that th' grasshoppers
    has got to hop three times to break even .....
    You couldn't raise an argument on it.

I got a gal just through the slew,
Everybody calls her Shotgun Sue —
Shoots off at her mouth and full of wind,
She's a pretty good gal for the shape she's in.
    Her land is so rich that the fruit trees wear the
    apples out waving them around in the air,
    Vines wears the watermelons out a-draggin'
    them around over the patch .....
    Grass grows so high on her place that she goes
    in the hole 'cause she cain't find her farm .....

# LUMBER IS KING

Words by Woody Guthrie
Music by Pete Seeger

1. I'm tree top Tom I'm a tree top - ping man, I top the tall tim - ber all

ov - er this land, It's buck - ing them up and it's snak - ing them down, cause

lum - ber is king in a lum - ber - ing town. I fell the might - y Doug - las and

tall spar tree, I buck 'em and raft 'em on down to the sea, It's

ties and rough lum - ber for the whole world 'round, 'cause

lum - ber is king in a lum - ber - ing town.

My father before me a logger was he,
He cleared all the forests in Minnesotee;
My grandfather logged it from Maine on down,
And Lumber is King in a Lumbering town.
    I'm 200 pound, and I'm six foot tall,
    At pulling my axe I'm the best of you all;
    One swing of my axe and a forest comes down;
    'Cause Lumber is King in a Lumbering Town.

Back in the 20's I worked every day,
It's $14 I drawed for my pay;
With women and drinking my sorrows I'd drown,
'Cause Lumber is King in a Lumbering Town.
    The Timber towns boomed in the year '29;
    A billion board feet of the fir and the pine;
    In 19 and 30 the mill shut down,
    'Cause Lumber is King in a Lumbering town.

Folks didn't buy timber for houses or mines,
The railroad was idle and didn't buy ties;
I was out of a job when the season come 'round'
'Cause Lumber is King in a Lumbering town.
    I hit up the bosses, but business was slow,
    So I hit the skids on the old Skid Row,
    I panhandled up and I panhandled down,
    'Cause Lumber is King in a Lumbering town.

Times are better the paper it shows,
Cutting the timber twice fast as it grows;
The trees will be gone when the years roll 'round,
'Cause Lumber is King in a Lumbering town.
    Fires and Varmints and insects and pests,
    The mechanical fellers will cut out the rest,
    Old 'high lead' logging is on it's way down,
    'Cause Lumber is King in a Lumbering town.

Folks from the plains, and folks from the east,
Folks from the Dust bowl that's struck with th' breeze,
Wanting to work, and no work to be found;
'Cause Lumber is King in a Lumbering town.
    What you gonna do 'bout these hard working men,
    Whole families, and women, and kids pouring in?
    Looking for land, and there's land to be found'
    But Lumber is King in a Lumbering town.

There's metals and min'ral hid out in them hills,
There's aluminum, chrome, and there's manganese mills;
Factories and shops that whistle and pound,
But Lumber is King in a Lumbering town.
 The big trees are falling, and us lumberjacks,
 With high power saw, and with double blade axe,
 It's fast diesel cats that's a bringing her down;
 'Cause Lumber is King in a Lumbering town.

But, think of the day when the land is cut o'er
And what of King Lumber when Timber's no more?
It's bright shining ore that you'll dig in the ground;
'Cause Lumber's Just King in a Lumbering town.
 Takes a flat thousand years for a big tree to grow,
 So I won't be cutting the next growth or so;
 A little too long for me to wait 'round;
 'Cause Lumber's Just King in a Lumbering town.

But, where can I go? What'll I do?
Where ever I went it would be the same, too;
No use in me a chasin' a rainbow around;
'Cause Lumber's Just King in a Lumbering town.
 I'll stick in the land that you call the Northwest,
 Where Lumber's still King, but King less and less,
 There's iron and there's copper and gold in this ground'
 And Lumber's just King in a Lumbering town.

We ain't got the coal Pennsylvania's got;
An' we ain't got the oil like Texas has got;
But the use of light metal is just coming 'round;
And Lumber's Just King in a Lumbering town.
 When old King Lumber's asleep in his grave,
 The Royal Chinook leap the white ocean wave,
 To the great King Columbia's spawning ground;
 'Cause Lumber's Just King in a Lumbering town.

And there at the rapids the great logging jams
Will go with the sawdust. Great Power Dams,
Grand Coulee. Umatilla. Bonneville. Down.
'Cause Lumber's just King in a Lumbering town.
 To me, an old axeman, it ain't so surprising;
 One King a dying, and another King rising;
 I knowed all along that it had to come 'round;
 'Cause Lumber's just King in a Lumbering town.

King Lumber might live for 100 years, too,
If when you cut one tree, you stop to plant 2;
But, Boys, if you don't, he's on his way down;
'Cause Lumber's just King in a Lumbering town.
 Uncle Sam needs me, Uncle Sam needs you;
 I'll outwork Paul Bunion and John Henry, too;
 I'll log in the timber, I'll mine in the ground;
 'Cause a Working Man's king in a Working Man's town.

# GUYS ON THE GRAND COULEE DAM

Words by Woody Guthrie
Music traditional ("Widdicombe Fair"),
arranged by Pete Seeger

1. O come a - long down the riv - er with me,

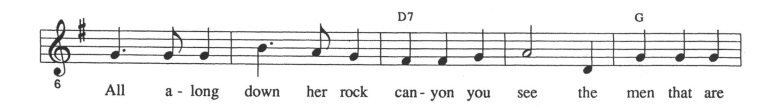

All a - long down her rock can - yon you see the men that are

build - ing your Grand Cou - lee Dam. Bill Jones, Pete

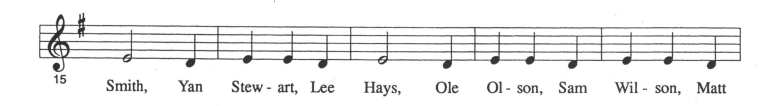

Smith, Yan Stew - art, Lee Hays, Ole Ol - son, Sam Wil - son, Matt

Jen - nings, Ed Wheel - er, Old Un - cle John Turn - er and

all_____ Old Un - cle John Turn - er and all.

We come a long ways, it was looking for work,
All along down the wide highway you see,
And this loafing 'round idle is really what hurts
 Bill Jones, Pete Smith, Yan Stewart, Lee Hays,
 Ole Olson, Sam Wilson, Matt Jennings, Ed Wheeler,
 Old Uncle John Turner and all, Old Uncle John Turner and all.


It's hard sweatin', hard fightin', hard workin' men,
All along down on Grand Coulee you'll see;
Blasting the canyon and damming her in,
 Bill Jones, Pete Smith, Yan Stewart, Lee Hays,
 Ole Olson, Sam Wilson, Matt Jennings, Ed Wheeler,
 Old Uncle John Turner and all, Old Uncle John Turner and all.


Bill Jones sets his powder a hundred feet deep
All along down in the bed rock and fires,
Pete Smith he sticks onto the sidewall so steep,
 Bill Jones, Pete Smith, Yan Stewart, Lee Hays,
 Ole Olson, Sam Wilson, Matt Jennings, Ed Wheeler,
 Old Uncle John Turner and all, Old Uncle John Turner and all.


Yan Stewart he laughs as his jackhammer plays
Through the deep tunnel, Ole Olson, Lee Hays;
Electric lights turn all the nights into days for
 Bill Jones, Pete Smith, Yan Stewart, Lee Hays,
 Ole Olson, Sam Wilson, Matt Jennings, Ed Wheeler,
 Old Uncle John Turner and all, Old Uncle John Turner and all.


Bonneville's done, next the Grand Coulee Dam
All along down where the Columbia she rolls,
It's more light and power for old Uncle Sam,
 (and) Bill Jones, Pete Smith, Yan Stewart, Lee Hays,
 Ole Olson, Sam Wilson, Matt Jennings, Ed Wheeler,
 Old Uncle John Turner and all, Old Uncle John Turner and all.

# THE BALLAD OF JACKHAMMER JOHN

Words by Woody Guthrie
Music adapted by Pete Seeger
(from the traditional song "House of the Rising Sun")

1. I went down to that ta-vern that you call the Ri-sing Sun. And what do you rec-kon that I saw? I seen Mis-ter Paul Bun-yan deal-in' cards to Dril-ler Drake, John Hen-ry and Jack-ham-mer John. Then the pret-ti-est lit-tle girl in this whole wide world, red, white, an' a blue bon-net on, poured a bar-rel for Mis-ter Bun-yan and a bar-rel for Mis-ter Drake, John Hen-ry and Jack-ham-mer John. Paul Bun-ion hol-lered I'm the man that

cuts the tim - ber in your land E - ver town in the good old U. S. A. All the

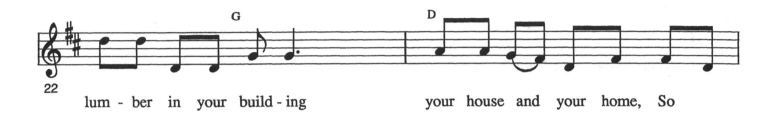

lum - ber in your build - ing your house and your home, So

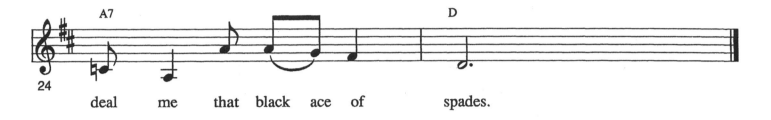

deal me that black ace of spades.

Driller Drake yelled, I'm th' boomer drills th' oil in all your land,
Pennsylvania, th' Great Lakes, and Gulf;
I keep your engine a'runnin', keep your wheels just slick as grease;
So deal me that little deuce of clubs.

John Henry roared, I'm the workinest of them steel drivin' men,
Chicago, and Birmin'ham, an say,
It's railroads, battleships, an' automobiles an' nail;
(Jack o' diamond is a hard card to play).

Then the Pretty Little Girl in the Red White & Blue
Says, it's nine hundred fact'ries that I run,
And a workin in the store, keepin' house next door,
And a-raisin' up a daughter and a son.

Yes, Jackhammer John took the Girly by the hand,
He sung, Well, I laid the pavement in your town,
Skyscrapers, tunnels, and bridges and dams,
(So you can deal me hole card down).


Oh, th' TVA in the State of Tennessee,
Muscle Shoals I knocked a hole in th' ground;
On the Boulder or the Butte with my hammer spittin fire;
It's power makes your wheels go 'round,


Mr. Bunion, you're the best of all them Lumberjacks,
You're a man that I always did admire,
But when your trees run low, and your axe is laid to rest,
Well you can hear my jack hammer spittin' fire;


Driller Drake, you're the best of them oil drillin' men,
And your friendship I highly desire;
But when your oil boom's over, and your bit's laid away,
Well, you can hear my jack hammer spittin' fire!


John Henry, you're the Man of them steel drivin' men;
But in the graveyard you will retire;
You gonna work so hard that you'll break your pore heart;
And you can hear my Jackhammer spittin' fire;


Paul Bunion he roared and he spit across the floor,
And then he grabbed up his axe in his hand;
Hollered, Jackhammer man, you done said too much;
You caint insult a wood choppin' man!


Driller Drake then spake like the rumble of a quake,
And his face was like a blizzard on the plain;
He said, Jackhammer John, get ready for your maker,
'Cause you caint make fun of a oil drillin' man!


John Henry grabbed the handle of a 20 pound sledge,
Pulled a 6 inch razor in his hand,
Said, Lord God, Boy, Mister Jackhammer John,
You cant be-little a steel drivin' man!

Then it was Jackhammer John grabbed the handle of his gun,
And his air hose commenced to suckin' wind;
Said, if I go to see my sweet eternity,
I got my tickets for three other men!


Then the hard workin' girl she jumped between the men,
Said, don't kill my Jackhammer John;
He might not of meant every word that he said,
He's a high temper man when he's young!


Then a sweet brown woman walked in at the door,
Said, my name's John Henry's Polly Ann,
If this is the place that you call the Risin' Sun,
I'm a lookin for my steel drivin man!


And the pretty little girl she opened up her mouth
And her was a ringin' like a bell,
You hard workin' men caint never make the grade
By squabblin' and fightin' 'mongst yourselves!


Paul Bunion grab your axe an' hit that timber trail,
Up where the mountain is blue;
And everytime you swing your axe a forest will fall,
You can dig a hole and plant back two.


Driller Drake hit the trail for the oil boomin' field,
It's oil makes the engine go around;
It's oil for the ships of the sea and the sky,
So don't waste a drop on the ground.


Jackhammer John got a dam buildin' job.
For the factories of good old Uncle Sam,
Makin A-lu-minum in the state of Washington,
From the power of the Grand Coulee Dam.


Well he thought of Paul Bunion when he seen the lumber used;
Driller Drake when he heard the engines run;
John Henry when he seen them cold steel beams,
And the tavern called the Rising Sun.

# PORTLAND TOWN TO KLAMATH FALLS

Words by Woody Guthrie
Music traditional ("The Crawdad Song"),
arranged by Pete Seeger

1. Well, I come from a Tex-as town, did-n't I ba-by?

Well, I come from a Tex-as to-wn, did-n't I ba-by?

That old dust it blowed and blowed, and I hit the lone-some road,

Lan-ded up in a Port-lan' to-wn, did-n't I ba-by?

I gotta gal in Klamath Falls, aint I, Baby?
I gotta gal in Klamath Falls, aint I, Baby?
Well, she's long, yes, she's tall,
Like the timber when she falls,
I gotta gal in Klamath Falls, aint I, Baby?

Klamath Falls is a railroad town, aint it, Baby?
Klamath Falls is a railroad town, aint it, Baby?
Klamath Falls is a railroad town,
You can ride the rattler down;
Klamath Falls is a railroad town, aint it, Baby?

Get your ticket and you come down, caint you, Baby?
Get your ticket and you come down, caint you, Baby?
Well it shore gits mighty lonesome
When that evenin' sun goes down,
Get your ticket and you come down, caint you, Baby?


You're a livin' in Portlan' town, aint you, Baby?
You're a livin' in Portlan' town, aint you, Baby?
Klamath Falls is a railroad town,
But I dont want no switchin' around;
Get your ticket and come on down, caint you, Baby?


Portlan' town is a shippin' town, aint it, Baby?
Portlan' town is a shippin' town, aint it, Baby?
I got a gal that's 6 foot aroun'
Tryin' to make a livin' in a shippin' town,
Portlan' town is a shippin' town, aint it, Baby?


Portlan' town is a timber town, aint it, Baby?
Portlan' town is a timber town, aint it, Baby?
When we raft that timber down,
And my payday rolls around;
I'm a goin' down to Klamath Falls to see my Baby.


I'm a gonna ride that railroad down to see my Baby,
I'm a gonna ride that railroad down to see my Baby;
Boy, she's long and she's tall,
She's th' best in Klamath Falls;
So I'm a gonna ride that railroad down to see my Baby.

# THE WHITE GHOST TRAIN

Words by Woody Guthrie
Music traditional ("Wabash Cannonball")

1. You have heard a-bout the fast-est trains that run from coast to coast

And you've sung a-bout the en-gin-neers and heard the peo-ple boast

the stream-line Chief and Ka-ty and the light-ning can-non ball,

But the train that's called the White Ghost train's the fast-est one of all.

Steaming through the foggy midnight, whistling down the silver rails,
Through the northern icy blizzard in the sleet and snow she sails,
When she throttles west to Texas there the springtime blooms again
Through the land of Desert Blossoms on the mighty White Ghost Train.

When a man and wife get married and are sleeping side by side
Dreaming pretty dreams of heaven, into California glide,
When the honeymoon its over and they both wake up again,
Well, its tickets then for Reno on the same old White Ghost Train.

Now the White Ghost Train is crowded and she runs around the world,
The rich and stingy miser and the loving boys and girls,
You can have your whirl at loving, and at trifling take a fling,
You will pull in Hell at midnight on the lovely White Ghost train.

She was foundered up in Boston, and the first run that she run
Was from Birmingham to Portland and she beat the Rising Sun,
She was full of pretty women and of tall and handsome men,
But she disappeared at Loveloft and was never seen again.

Tell your darling sweetheart and tell your loving wife,
This train you call the White Ghost will take you down through life,
From the land of tender kisses, from the cradle to the grave
Then it's westward to Death Valley on the limited White Ghost train.

*SPOKANE — "Way back in 1940 or '41, I made a fast walking trip up and down the basin of the Columbia River and its tributaries, the Snake, the Hood, Willamette, Yakima and the Klickitat, making up little songs about what I seen. I made up 26 songs about the Bonneville Dam, Grand Coulee Dam, and the thunderous foamy waters of the rapids and cascades, the wild and windward watersprays from the high Sheliloh falls, and the folks living in thee little shack house just about a mile from the end of the line. The Department of Interior folks got a hold of me and took me into a clothes closet there at the Bonneville Power Administration house in Portland and melted my songs down onto records."*

Woody Guthrie

*"When a song or a ballad mentions the name of a river, a town, a spot, a fight, or the sound of somebody's name that you know and are familiar with, there is a sort of quiet kind of pride comes up through your blood. And if it is a true song about a true job of work, or about something that really did happen and which you had your hand in oh, well, then it gets to be something you grab the first thing if your house catches fire and there's not no water around. It lasts you through several suits of clothes, plays, dances, movies, and lasts you even on down through children, mates, wives and husbands.*

*These Pacific Northwest songs and ballads have got all of these personal feelings for me because I was there on these very spots and very grounds before, when the rock wall canyon stood there laughing around at me, and while the crazybug machines, jeeps, jacks, dozers, mixers, trucks, cars, lifts, chains and pulleys and all of us beat outselves down every day yelling and singing little snatches of songs we was too hot and too busy and too tired to set down with our pen and pencil right then while the thing was being built. This is the main thing I tried to get at here in these Pacific Northwest songs."*

Woody Guthrie